For more information, images or videos, please visit
The Dog in the Clouds web site at www.thedogintheclouds.com

———————————

*This story is for Roo, the bravest
puppy I ever knew.*

———————————

Notes from a Dog Rescue in Progress

Brian Beker

1

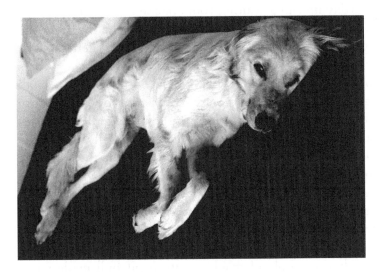

A beautiful young Golden Retriever is hiding in the dark in my closet. I have seen her eyes in the sunlight, so I know they are filled with fear. By the time I got her, all she wanted was a place where she could hide her head. She scrambled behind the toilet. Eventually I cleared a den for her in the back of a closet. She is shutting out a world in which everything scares her. I hear her shallow panting.

Roo was named by a rescue worker from Independent Labrador Retriever Rescue of Southern California who pulled her from a high-kill shelter in Los Angeles and brought her to an inner-city clinic to be spayed. The first time I saw her, she was trembling at the end of a leash when a tech brought her out into a Saturday morning waiting room packed with pit bulls and Chihuahuas. The tech was downcast about the state the dog was in, or maybe just about the job in general. His scrubs were bloody, and Roo was covered in a week's worth of what happens when you're not let out of a small cage. The amount of money vouchered by the county didn't inspire anyone to rinse the thick wadding of feces and urine off this girl before slicing her belly open. The golden fur bred into her by humans for their luxury requires human grooming. Roo's was the dirty grey of the LA streets. It was gnarled into dreadlocks made of a hardened mixture of cement and gravel. The sides of her abdomen were sucked in tight. She didn't walk so much as stumble. As soon as she got outside, she peed for so long that a couple of machos with a pit bull made some cracks her way. I gave them a look that could have made me a gang casualty. Their pit bull looked like a kind dog with his own problems.

She was terrified, but Roo still had her dignity. More than I could say for myself some of the times when I've been wounded, scared, filthy, friendless and left for dead. I fell a little in love with her.

Sounds that I couldn't even hear sent Roo cringing to ground, her snout flattened in submission on the sidewalk. She expected everything to hurt her. In the bright sunlight I saw dozens of fleas crawling on her. I got down on the sidewalk and felt her trembling when I held her. She let me. With my body against hers I felt her irregular breathing. I tried to tell her things were looking up, but I don't know if I sounded convincing.

The idea of getting in the car terrified her. I lifted her up and put her in. Every muscle in her body was as tense as a high-voltage wire. She froze and shook.

My guess is that this dog had been imprisoned. She probably grew up in a cage or a bathroom. It would explain why going into a house would be so threatening to her. Pulling on her leash wasn't an option. I picked her up to bring her inside. For a minute I just held her and before long her muscles softened and her head drooped onto my arm. There are times a dog needs to be held as much as any human does.

Her crooked incision was inelegantly stitched. It looked like a homemade carpet repair. She was in no state to eat or drink, and what courage she worked up she used to scramble for a spot to hide. She jammed herself behind the toilet. I once knew a dog who marched himself up on top of a garbage pile when he was ready to die. It was heartbreaking. Roo reminded me of him.

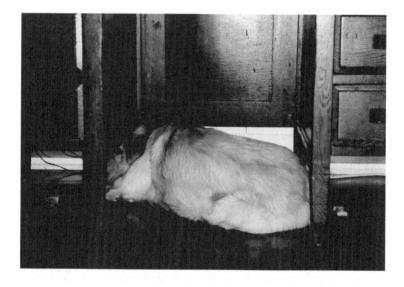

But I knew something Roo didn't know. I knew that her days of being harmed are over.

On balance, humans don't have much to be proud of in the way we breed dogs and dictate the conditions of their lives as our property. Instead of living up to our simple end of the bargain - the provision of food, shelter and care - we are all too prone to letting those dependent lives be destroyed. Beings who start out pure and hopeful have their spirits crushed by what would be bad luck if it wasn't entirely man-made. Well-loved dogs who are blessed with good lives comprise a tiny minority. Dogs like Roo - neglected, scared, jettisoned, sick and starved - are everywhere.

Any shelter is filled with dogs at every stage of the decline. Fur rots and tangles and becomes home to parasites before it falls out in clumps. Skeletons show. Infected ears make every moment a hell of pain and itching - under Roo's flaps it's all hot red swelling and thick brown wax. The skin is covered with sores from malnutrition and bloody scabs from gnawing at the fleas. Cuts fester. Teeth turn brown. Scars accumulate. Limps develop. Those are just the visible things. Those can be treated.

Fear is a much tougher customer.

The fear is what you see in Roo's deep brown eyes. Once she was a puppy whose eyes smiled at everything she saw. On her journey to her hiding spot behind a toilet, those smiles were extinguished.

My work was cut out for me. First things first - fleas and filth had to be dealt with so Roo could start to heal. Her incision could not be made wet, so a real bath was out of the question. Even if the incision could be protected, the flea meds can't be applied after a shampoo.

After letting her decompress for an hour or so behind the toilet I pulled her out as softly as I could and carried her outside. I showed her how the hose works - it didn't bother her - and ran a slow stream of cool water over her. I don't have a bathtub, so that was the only choice. The thick black infestation of flea eggs on her back would have to wait; the water would have run down onto her belly.

Roo held still and began to close her eyes as the water ran over her. I worked as much of the dirt out of her with my hands as I could. She never moved an inch, and when the water soaked through the fur on her head I felt her take a deep breath and relax the muscles in her neck. Her head lowered a bit, and I felt her tongue lick my arm, tentatively and only a couple of times. I know what is feels like to receive unexpected kindness from someone who cares when you are wounded and frightened. Roo was feeling what I had felt. Cool water on a hot day. Sometimes it takes so little to help. I patted her soft golden mane down with a towel. For a moment, with fleas crawling around a spot on her snout that she had scratched raw, she raised her eyes to look into mine. Her eyes were filled with exhaustion and strain, but for that moment there was no fear. Her look made me stop and hold her and she moved closer and leaned the top of her head against me.

Balls of cement mixed with sharp rocks were jammed in-between her footpads and underneath her claws. No wonder she had been walking gingerly. I chopped all the worst of it off with scissors. When I finished with one paw, she offered the other.

If it was true that Roo had suffered long imprisonment, it would account for why she was scared to come back inside the house. But back inside, she chose a spot under the desk instead of cramming herself behind the toilet, and that was a little less heartbreaking. At least she had chosen to be in the same room. It was a start.

She didn't want any food or water. She just wanted to sleep. I left her in peace. I couldn't take my eyes off her.

After a couple of hours I got down on my hands and knees to say hi to her and see if she might take a sip of water. Though she wasn't ready for that, the tip of her tail tapped the floor a couple of times when she saw me. It wasn't much of a wag as wags go, but it was as much of a wag as this weakened dog could work up, and it practically brought tears to my eyes. It was one of the best wags ever. I held her head in my hands, and she went to sleep like that, her soft lips on the palm of my hand. And I felt her take a breath so deep that her ribs pushed up against mine. She sighed it out in that jagged way human children do at the end of a heavy cry.

Roo needs to have basic needs met. Fleas, recovery, nutrition. Her ears. Her coat. Above all, Roo needs love and kindness. I have my work cut out for me. Whatever someone did to the angel in the tattered golden coat needs to be undone.

I'm almost as scared as she is.

2

Some things that have made Roo run for her life:

A paint bucket.
The sound of a light switch flipping.
Drawers opening.
A paper clip falling on the floor.
Leaves rustling on trees.
A hose lying on the ground.
Footsteps.

What little I knew of Roo's journey up to the day I met her was not encouraging.

Her official history only goes back a few weeks to when she was brought in as a stray to a high-kill shelter in Los Angeles. Caged, she deteriorated. Her fur was falling out and her skin was damaged. She was heavily infested with fleas. Ticks were buried in her face and neck. Her skeleton showed. Walking was painful. Worst of all was her mental state. She had been described by the Indi Lab Rescue volunteer who found her as, "the most petrified Golden I've ever seen."

Sounds only she could hear made her drop to the ground. She spent her first night trembling in a closet. Turning on a light was torture to her and only made her try to squeeze her face into a corner. I left her in the dark and looked in on her every hour or so. Mostly I spent the night scared to move.

I heard her panting and scratching, and the fear I created whenever she saw me made me more convinced that I wasn't up to the task of helping a dog this far gone. But there was no point. I was all Roo was going to get. In the shelter she was a cringing skeleton in rags who wouldn't trot up to anyone with her tail wagging. She didn't stand much of a chance of getting adopted before her number was placed on the kill list. It was either a volunteer foster like me, up to the task or not, or in a few days a terrified Roo would be forced out of her cage and wrestled onto a cold steel table. She would have had to be restrained hard to get a needle in her arm for the overdose of barbiturates. Rescue is just regular people doing the best they can to keep a few needles out of the arms of a few Roos. Not always a perfect reprieve.

After her night in the closet Roo looked like a pile of rags. She wouldn't eat and barely dipped the tip of her tongue in a bowl of water. The Frontline application from the day before still hadn't polished off the fleas, and she was running out of the energy to scratch herself. Every time she lifted a paw she got lost deciding what to itch and dropped it.

I waited until morning light to join her on the floor of the closet. After a few minutes with her I took a whiff of her ears. They couldn't be allowed to keep festering. I brought the ear cleaning supplies over and let Roo smell everything. The crinkling noise of the plastic bag the cotton balls were in startled her. I soaked one with otic solution and raised an ear flap. I was surprised that she only tensed a little. The cotton took on the sticky consistency of dirty clay after a few dips. I worked on both ears for about five minutes, and put Neosporin on the pink skin she had scratched raw. The relief was instant. She was able to drink some water and eat a piece of turkey the size of a quarter. She sighed and put her head down. I left her alone to sleep.

A couple of hours later a sound like someone shaking a cardboard box full of bones came from the closet. Before I could get there, Roo stumbled out into the room tripping over herself, trying to bite at her whole body at once, standing, falling, batting at her eyes with her front paws, chewing at her arms, twisting to bite her back. Her face was under the worst assault - she clawed at it frantically.

Fleas were crawling in and out of her eyes. They were all over her snout and squirming in and out of her eyebrows. Eighteen hours after applying the flea meds it seemed to have made it worse. Later I would learn that the Frontline makes fleas hyperactive before they die. At the time, it just appeared that Roo, who wasn't waterproof and couldn't take a bath with her fresh incision, was being bitten to death.

I led her outside into the light and picked them from her eyes and snout. She flung her head around wildly for a minute, but then something changed, as if one of the switches she was scared of had been flipped. Roo made the kind of decision that powers the bond between dogs and humans. She stopped struggling and held her face toward me. The connection was made.

Eventually she was able to calm a little.

Roo was ready to let me inspect her more closely. Flea eggs were so thick on her pink skin that in places it looked like road tar. She had scabs and sores everywhere from picking at herself. She had chewed through the skin on her forearms.

She had much more concrete all over her body than I had seen. It bunched up and pulled strands of her hair into tight knots on her belly, sides, tail, and all the way up to the inside of her groin. She let me snip at them. The worst were spiky pebbles between her footpads and in between her toes, some thick enough to spread them. The way she had been favoring each of her paws with every step had looked like general weakness, but this would explain it. She let me work on them a little, but to get it all out would take more patience than she had just yet.

She enjoyed a brisk brushing. Working back and forth against the grain of her coat helped rustle away flea eggs. In the fine hairs of her underside, the brush hit tangles of concrete, and I chopped them out. As hurt and weary as she was, she was completely cooperative. There was a grace and dignity to the way she accepted the help that moved me. A little of her natural golden tone began to shine past the grey.

Throughout all of this Roo had to battle her fear. She was being handled while noise made her cringe. Holding her and cooing at her seemed to help. Whatever had been done to her, she was already showing signs of willingness to give another human another chance.

Roo's age had been listed as three years old. Presumably by professionals. The dark brown of her teeth was enough to convince anyone of that. But the more I looked at her, the less I believed it. She was starting to look much younger.

The day before, going into the house terrified Roo, but now she returned on her own. She went on a slow nose patrol and found something that interested her jammed into a low shelf and gingerly tugged on it. It was a stuffed toy, a mallard I had bought for my last foster, who ignored it.

Roo limped towards the closet with the stuffed goose in her mouth. Before she got there she stopped and turned her head to me. She seemed to think about things a little. With that goose still in her mouth, she put her chin up on the bed. I don't care about that old chestnut about lying down with dogs and getting up with fleas. Small price to pay. I got my arms under her, and put her up on the bed. She dropped the goose and lay down beside it.

The phone rang, making Roo jump. I decided to

try something. I put an arm around her - with no hint of restraint - switched the ringer off and moved the phone closer to her, saying, "It's okay, Roo. It's okay, puppy," turned the ringer back on for an instant and off. She sniffed at it and calmed down quickly. I did it a couple of times, and the noise stopped scaring her. If she had been locked up her whole life, every sound was new to her. That she could learn this quickly that something wasn't a threat was good news.

She went right to sleep and slept through the rest of the day and into the night. I left the ringer off just in case.

The next morning when she woke up and found me looking at her, she thumped her tail on the bed. She reached her paws towards me and wiggled a couple of inches closer and stretched her neck out to sniff me. She gave me a few licks on the arm and smiled.

This was no three-year-old. This was someone neglected, locked up, deprived of experience. This was a puppy, someone with brown teeth because she never got anything to chew. Someone who might have been tossed into the street when she chewed something she wasn't supposed to. But not at three.

I helped Roo off the bed and outside. She needed to walk even if she didn't want to. Pain and fear made her stop every few steps. Encouragement got her going again.

A neighbor was pushing a child in a stroller out of their house. The little girl in the stroller was about seven. She had cerebral palsy and a big smile for Roo. She said, "Can I touch the puppy?" Roo put her ears up and inched towards her.

The little girl kept talking to Roo. She was such a pretty kid. Roo sniffed her. Her tail went from side to side two or three times and the little girl tried to place her hand on Roo's head. The uncertainty of the motion made Roo duck, but then she came back up and held still, and the girl got her hand on Roo's head. She screamed with delight, which I thought would send Roo flying, but she just looked at the girl, who kept her hand on the dog's head. Her mother wasn't as much of a fan of dogs as the kid was. She wheeled her away.

We had walked enough. Back inside Roo ate a few bites of turkey, drank a few sips of water and lay down on the floor. I spent a little time telling her what a great dog she was. She liked that. When I showed her the scissors and held one of her paws and took a snip at the concrete she didn't argue.

Half an hour later, every last bit of concrete was out of Roo's paws and fur and in a pile on the floor. I was anxious to see how she would walk, but she didn't want to move. She gave me a few licks like a puppy would. I had a strong feeling that this was a young dog who had been disguised as an older one by dark brown teeth, a limp, a raggedy coat and above all none of the happiness you would expect to see in a puppy's expression.

The younger she was, the better her chances would be. It was the beginning of Day Three. I was starting to get my hopes up.

3

After a few days, Roo had a lot to feel better about.

The flea infestation was gone. Her sores and wounds were healing. There was no more concrete between her toes. Her coat was free of tangles and filth. Now that she was eating again, her young body was soaking up nutrients and putting on weight. The sludge of wax in her ears that had made her scratch herself bloody under the flaps was gone, and the fair skin was turning pink again. She needed a lot of sleep and was getting it. In less than a week Roo started to look like a new dog. Most importantly, her spirit had survived the abuse and neglect. She wagged and smiled more each day.

But you can't treat fear with food or salve, and fear was the only injury threatening to scar Roo permanently. Unexpected noises frightened her more than anything. It helped to keep everything as quiet as possible. Without adrenaline coursing through her body all the time she was finally able to relax. But then even the smallest sound would pierce the delicate calm and send Roo back into a panic. In an instant she would go from sleep to scrambling for cover, slipping on the floor, cramming herself under a chair or into a corner. Terrorized.

I was on pins and needles, obsessing about not making even the smallest noises. I tried not to let dishes clank or closet doors squeak. When I took a shoe off I placed it gingerly on the floor. I learned to put a pen down carefully. But the more you try to eliminate the sounds of everyday life, the more of them you realize there are. Silence was unattainable. With every move I made I tightened up more. I was sure that my tension affected Roo. It was a classic feedback loop.

Roo's fear - analyzing it, trying to understand it -

became my preoccupation.

My theory that she had been confined would explain why so many things scared her. Her experience of sudden noises might not have begun until she was hauled out of a closet and dumped in the streets or dragged into the shelter. She would never have had the chance to figure anything out. The fear never subsided, it was only being ramped up by the bombardment of new stimuli. Everything was associated with terror. Roo was stretched to the breaking point. It was a miracle she hadn't broken.

Some things, like shadows and reflections, worried her but didn't panic her. Those could wait.

Other things were easy to see and avoid. A hand on a door, for example. Roo must have been used to being thrown into a closet or a bathroom with a door slammed to trap her. If I held the door when it was time to come inside, Roo stopped dead in her tracks, stared at my hand and prepared to bolt. As soon as I stood clear she would come through. No more hands on the door.

Roo with Donna Salvini, selfless rescuer, founder of Independent Labrador Rescue of Southern California, and the woman who called one day to assign a frightened foster named Roo to me. With Brandon, a chocolate Labrador who was the victim of years of violent abuse. He trusts only Donna.

Sudden noises were the main trouble. When the sound of some dental floss pulling off the reel made Roo jump up and try to hide her face under the couch, it made me so sad for her suffering that I had to try something. Anything. Silence had been a restorative for Roo, but it wasn't a long-term answer. I didn't have the power to silence the world - even the world inside this one-room house - for her. It was time for us to take a next step together.

I waited until Roo was calm again. She lay on the bed. I slid open a kitchen drawer and took out the silverware tray. She watched with curiosity. Kitchen things could signal good news, after all. I brought the tray over to her and placed it slowly on the bed. The strange object caused her to tense up a little and look away.

"It's okay, puppy girl," I said. She sniffed it.

Any time over the past few days that something scared Roo I tried to comfort her by holding her and cooing that we weren't afraid of noises, that noises wouldn't hurt us, that big puppies don't care about noises. I lay beside her and kept a protective arm around her, with a hand on her chest, which I knew she liked because she always leaned into me when I did it. I went on for a long time telling her what a brave girl she was and how proud of her I was and how I wouldn't let anything hurt her. How she was going to be just like all the other dogs, better in ways, because the strength of spirit and the dignity that had carried her so far would guide her on to the life of a great dog. I can really go on when I'm talking to a dog.

Slowly I moved my hand to the tray and took the spoon at the bottom of the stack, which made for some jangling when I lifted it. Just enough to frighten Roo. "It's okay, big puppy, just a noise, just a noise.... We don't care about noises, Roo Kahoo...."

Roo positioned her paws to bolt - but didn't. With the spoon free of the tray, just a silent object in my hand, I moved it towards her nose so she could sniff it. "You see, puppy? It's just a spoon!" I felt her muscles in her shoulders relax the tiniest bit. "Watch this, puppy girl," I said, trying to sound playful, and I put the spoon back in the tray with a clink. Her eyes were wide and her ears were up. She was paying attention.

If Roo was any judge of tone of voice, she knew I meant every word of what I was saying about what a great dog she was, about how I loved her and how brave I thought she was. I repeated the process of making little clinking sounds a few times. All the tension went out of her. And in a few seconds, that was that. I clanked the silverware around some more and she started to close her eyes to get back to sleep.

Roo wasn't scared of the sound of a spoon any

more. With an understanding of that one noise, the fear of it vanished.

Roo took it in her stride, but for me it was one of the greatest experiences I ever had with a dog. A lightning-fast lesson and a complete success. If she could learn that one she could learn them all. For the first time since the petrified girl had come home with me I felt real hope.

I pulled her up by the arms up to roll her on her back - a game she enjoyed - and rubbed her belly and bicycled her paws and hugged her and played with her and got her laughing.

What I saw sure wasn't the laugh of the three-year-old they thought she was at the shelter. She was starting to look younger all the time.

This was the laugh of a puppy. Desperation made her look like an older dog. Healing was making her look younger.

I took the tray back to the kitchen drawer and dropped it the last inch into the drawer. Not so much as a blink. The accomplishment didn't seem to be a big deal to Roo. She was already getting back to sleep. I was surprised at how moved I was. Trust, intelligence, bravery, and the openness necessary to relate to a human - some of the best things about dogs rolled up into the puppy lying on the bed.

I was tempted to keep going, to click the switch of the bedside light and to show that to her, too, but got ahold of myself. I watched her sleep. Golden indeed. She seemed to glow, and I watched her for a long time.

❈   ❈   ❈

Roo hangs out with other Indi Lab rescues at the dog park.

Fostering dogs is a combination of heartbreak and joy. People ask if it isn't heartbreaking when they're adopted, and for me the answer is not really, because I know they're off to realize their lives where they'll be better off in a bigger pack, with more humans, more space, other dogs.

For me, the heartbreak starts long before there's any question of giving them up, before I even lay eyes on them. It starts at the shelters, where, in Los Angeles, limitations on space dictate that "unadoptables" make room for new arrivals. Hundreds of sound dogs - from puppies and pit bulls to purebreds - deemed unadoptable as soon as they arrive - are killed all day every day. They are dying right now as you read this. A hard-fought new law gives animals four days to live from the time they're checked in, up from none. If you believe in the capabilities of dogs as I do, then you believe that that last bit of their time on Earth is filled with the smells of death and fear.

It's heartbreaking just standing in the long lines at the shelters. Heartbreak arrives in the cars that pull up. It is clear in the eyes of the dogs who are manhandled into cages by humans who make it easy on themselves by telling shelter staff that they're just bringing in a stray. It is hard to look at those dogs as their humans walk away. Of course they are confused. A dog would never throw someone away. You wonder what kind of person is able to not look back, but you know the answer. It's people, after all, who are responsible for the endless tide of puppies who wash up on the streets and in the cages. Dogs who never get a medication until the last minute of their lives.

The joy follows moments later with the freeing of an animal. Rescue doesn't account for a fraction of a percentage point's worth of difference in a place like LA. But it makes all the difference in the world to the one saved.

It also makes all the difference in the world to the rescuer.

The joy is in that first walk and in watching them take the long pees they always do. It is in leading them away from the barking and shrieking echoing off the cinderblock walls. The rescuer gets the deep pleasure of giving a deprived dog something good to eat. Of getting them to a safe place. Of cleaning them up. When the dog is ready to play again, we are the ones they play with. When they are ready to love a human again, we are the objects of it.

I watched Roo lying on the bed. She is the one who has to do all the hard parts. I am no hero and I am no saint and I have not done anything to merit the great gift of this time with her. I am someone who wasted space for years when it could have been used to save other Roos. I regret that. Other Roos didn't make it, when all it would have taken is an answer to the constant pleas for fosters from rescue groups.

❊   ❊   ❊

When Roo woke up from her nap, I got her interested in the stuffed mallard she chose for her own when she first arrived. She doesn't really know any games yet, but puppies like to play, and playing with it made her happy, though not nearly as happy as it made me. I mixed in some of the sounds that had been scaring her. The clicking switch on the lamp. The loud old light switches. I reeled off some dental floss and put a dish in the cupboard. She learned the sound of sticky drawers opening. She learned the sound of the broken old garage door and the sound of the pipes hissing in the house when the hose ran. If it bothered her, she did what retrievers do. She took it out on the mallard.

From a left-for-dead shelter dog to blossoming puppy in a week. There was a long way to go, but there was no stopping Roo now.

4

The first week with Roo was like a time-lapse film of a flower blossoming. Her ragged coat gained luster and thickness. She carried her head higher and perked up her ears. As her atrophied musculature improved, her limping became less noticeable. She became curious and started cautiously poking her nose into places she wouldn't go near before. The look of a cornered prey animal began to alternate with the smile of a puppy. Playing with her gave me the cover for teaching her about her world. The first time Roo saw a tennis ball she didn't know what it was, but there is a tennis ball gene in retriever DNA, and as soon as Roo saw one roll on the floor, she pounced on it. In minutes she was chasing it into the shadows that previously made her tuck her tail. The first time she caught a ball, she sported the proud posture of all dogs who make a good catch - the short trot with ears back and a modest wag. In no time she jumped gracefully three feet off the ground to snatch a ball out of the air. She was brave. She was beautiful. She was strong at heart.

Her improvement meant that it was time to start considering Roo's future placement in a permanent pack. Letting her go would be hard.

The first time Roo chanced putting her head out the window.

There were reminders that she had spent her life in confinement. Roo had no language skills, at least not in English or Spanish. It's easy to take the way our dogs understand us for granted, but in reality it is a magical gift that relies on a relationship with humans to develop. *Fast mapping*, a brain function used by toddlers and dogs, enables them to learn words at an extraordinary rate when they're young. When we love dogs we talk to them, which ameliorates the quality of their brain development. It makes the connection between humans and dogs uniquely powerful. It is the reason every admiring dog owner eventually brags that, "I swear that dog understands every word I say."

Isolated in a closet or bathroom, deprived of contact as much as she was of food, play, grooming or cleaning, medicine for her infections or wounds, flea protection or even just something to chew once in a while, Roo never got the chance to learn. It was a lingering sign of how blood-boilingly stupid and cruel her treatment had been.

Roo was close to wild when she got here. She looked feral and moved like a jackal. She understood nothing. I worried that some developmental window – some crucial period when a puppy needs to hear words and tones of voice in order to build the neural systems to acquire language – might have passed. Able to experience the world with more understanding, dogs with developed intellectual and physical capabilities are more confident and calm. Roo had as much right to that as any other dog. She had been cheated out of enough.

Roo and Brian. Photo by Jon Winokur.

Shy dogs avoid eye contact. I talked to Roo constantly, calling her name to get her to look at me. I cooed, "Roo-Roo-Roo" and "good girl" when she did. I rewarded every smile with affection and sang songs to her with some combination of her name and how much I loved her as the lyrics. I concocted opportunities for her to succeed constantly - following me, coming through a door, coming to me - so that I could praise her and back it up with play and petting. I chose a few words that paired with objects or events and repeated them a million times. *Cookie. Tennis ball. Ready. Bear. Walk. Hungry. Dog park. Jump. Play. Come, come in, come up. In the car.* And, of course, *Roo, Roo, Roo* all the time. Fun and affection were her ongoing rewards, and they worked wonders for this deprived puppy. The more proud and happy she made me, the more she felt the connection that makes humans and dogs the ultimate interspecies pair.

There is always that first time a dog looks at you when you call their name, and when Roo did, I practically smothered her. She began to come when called. She learned to sit to let me clip her leash on, which was a help, because otherwise the appearance of her leash made her hop around with puppyish glee and then flop on her side to make a wrestling match out of putting it on.

A week earlier the idea of taking this terror-stricken dog to a park would have been absurd. But now, it was at the dog park that Roo shined her brightest. Free of a leash, able to go where she wanted in a place without startling noises and in the company of other relaxed dogs, Roo forgot her troubles. She acted like a normal dog. Even her caution with people subsided. The first few minutes Roo was with the other dogs, she didn't seem sure of what they were doing or how to fit in, but soon she joined in running and chasing. Seeing her run so beautifully moved me. I couldn't take my eyes off her. She was learning to be a dog, and even though her atrophied muscles made her limp after a short time, this was strong medicine. We made the trips every day.

Roo was turning into a happy puppy who just happened to be a little nervous. She was learning constantly and gaining confidence. She was putting on a lot of weight. Sounds still made her jump, but they didn't make her bolt or drop cringing to the ground. It was hard to believe that a dog who appeared to have been as damaged as Roo was coming out of her shell so fast. Exactly two weeks after her arrival I put her on the scale at the pet store. Her shelter weight 16 days earlier was 49 pounds. Now she tipped the scales at just under 57.

Roo meets Jon Winokur, author of *Mondo Canine*, and Norrie Epstein, co-author with Jon of *Happy Motoring: Canine Life in the Fast Lane.*

I started to relax. Roo was smart and adaptable. She was healing. She would do well in the right home. Before long, Roo could make her debut on the Indi Labs web site. It was time - for her sake - to start looking for the pack that she would spend the rest of her life with. We would take as long as necessary to find the right family, with the experience and resources - and other dogs - to make sure Roo would continue to heal.

※　　　※　　　※

One night Roo had a setback.

She was lying on the bed chewing a bully stick. I was trying to get some work done on the computer, but I was distracted. Roo's eyes were half-closed and the muscles on the top of her head were getting a workout as she gnawed. I can't get enough of watching a dog chew. I was wondering if chewing would be enough to get the brown stains off her neglected teeth when the air conditioner quit.

Roo watched me take a flashlight - an item that used to panic her and now just made her back off - and go outside. She decided to stay behind with her chew. It was a welcome sign of her growing security. I went around the side of the house and climbed up to press the reset button on the unit. I went back inside the house. I had been gone no more than 30 seconds.

No Roo. I looked in the few spaces where she could be - the closet, the bathroom, but no Roo. I went back outside and called her. I shined the flashlight around until I found her at the gate. I switched it off as soon as I saw that she was in a full-blown state of panic, clawing at the steel, trying to get out to the street.

Her panic sent a jolt of adrenaline through me. I thought we had left the zone where everything scared Roo and I was always scared of scaring Roo. I approached slowly.

"Roo, girl, it's okay, puppy... Roo, Roo, puppy...," I said as I moved closer to her. It was pointless. Her heart was pounding, she was frantic and not capable of hearing anything. There was a weak part of the fence and she found it and started tearing at it and I had to get ahold of her. Touching her electrified her. She bolted in the opposite direction, across the courtyard to the door leading to the alley. She clawed at the rotting wood, at the pavement beneath it. She had made herself as small as she could to try to squeeze out the bottom. The walkway going to her was too narrow for both of us. I didn't want to corner her, but with the force of her panic she could get through that dilapidated old door, and if she did, she would take off into the nighttime traffic. I crept up on her slowly and got down in the dirt with her. I didn't know what to do other than try to hold her. Her body was hard as rocks and trembling, every muscle concentrating on pushing her head under the door. After a minute she stopped. We just sat there for a while.

What scared her so badly? She was in her own world, unresponsive, anguished. It was dark, but I knew she had her eyes pressed closed, the way she did on her first day.

Eventually I stood. A minute later, in what seemed like an act of sheer will, Roo got off the ground to an uneasy crouch, but something was too much for her. Her legs jerked back into motion and she ran again, this time back into the house. I got there a few seconds after her. She wasn't in sight.

I knew where she was. I went straight to the bathroom. For the first time since she arrived, when she was probably as scared as she had ever been, Roo was back behind the toilet, her head jammed out of sight.

Radiating loneliness, used to hiding in small spaces.

I took some time to think and to let Roo calm down. She reminded me of a time when I was just like her. Alone in the dirt on the floor of a 113-degree jungle on the other side of the world. Dried out, sick with dysentery, unable to move. Certain I was going to die and no ideas better than lying there and giving up. A man in a turban appeared and told me something that unlocked whatever that thing is that we all need help unlocking sometimes. It was the thing that got me out of the dirt and out of the jungle and back to life.

All the man in the turban said was: "If you proceed with courage, you will arrive without fail."

I didn't know how that lesson could apply to a dog, but it helped me then, and it was helping me now. I could only think of one thing to help Roo. Only one thing made any sense. Roo had begun to trust me. It was time to put that trust to work.

It was time for her to get the idea that if she proceeded with courage, she, too, would arrive without fail.

5

IN KAHOOTS

Right before something jolted Roo back into a state of terror, she was probably doing better than ever before in her life. The effects of the isolation and starvation that had characterized the first part of her puppyhood were fading. She was part of a pack - even if it was just a little pack of two - and she seemed to marvel in the idea that she had a friend. She was hungry for the guidance a puppy needs and cooperative when she understood it. Her body was toning rapidly as she learned to play and found the joy in running with other dogs, and every day she ran more and limped less. It was no wonder that shelter staff had estimated her to be three years old. Without the happy expressions and movements of a puppy, she looked much older. As she smiled more and became curious about things around her that had only frightened her before, she pounced and wiggled and wagged more. She looked younger all the time. Being a part of her progress was one of the most gratifying experiences of my life. I found it hard not to stare at her when she slept.

The night she was badly scared, Roo was

sprawled out on the bed, luxuriously gnawing on a bully stick. She looked at me frequently and thumped her tail a couple of times and gave me bright-eyed smiles. Contentment and having someone to communicate it to were as novel to her as being given something good to chew. I paid attention to every detail about Roo. When the air conditioner quit and I went outside to see check on it, I was glad to note that she felt secure enough to stay behind with her chew.

In the minute I was gone, something happened to send Roo into a panic. When I found her, she was distraught and frantically throwing herself against the gate so she could escape onto the street. When I got close to her, she ran back into the house and hid behind the toilet. Her claws were turned down into the tile and her body was as tight as a knot. Her panting was horrible to hear - sharp and impossibly fast, an anguished grunt with every exhalation. She was right back where she had started two weeks before.

There will never be any way to know what experiences had made her so frightened of the world. Someone might have found it amusing to taunt a puppy or rough one up or make her scamper with bright flashlights. The only thing she had learned was to expect the worst. She never even had the chance to gain the confidence developed in play. Everything was a threat to her, and she learned to respond in the only way a solitary puppy could - to bolt and hide and make herself as small as possible and try to shut the world out. Seeing her behind the toilet again was one of the most lonely things I've ever seen.

I knew how she felt. When I was young, I was crushed and knocked hard on the head. It left me confused about the simplest workings of the world. I also thought there was nothing to do but wait for bad things I didn't understand to pass. Later, when I became paralyzed with a tumor on the spinal cord, it seemed to prove that somehow I had failed to hide hard enough. I was just like Roo, running off and trying to become invisible in dark holes. My holes were dingy places in distant countries, but it was the same. Of course, the years wasted in hiding never did any good. Maybe, in some roundabout way, they could now, for Roo. If they could, it would make it all worthwhile.

All I had was the idea that something had to be done to give Roo the idea that there was a better way than to hide. I had no confidence about how to do it. I went to the front gate and opened it. When I came back, I picked up Roo's collar and leash and approached the bathroom jangling them, saying, "Come on, little puppy - time for a walk!"

She tried to claw her way farther behind the toilet,

but her shoulders and chest were already jammed as far as they would go against the porcelain.

"Come on, puppy girl - will you come for a walk with me?"

I couldn't sufficiently fake enough cool to be reassuring to Roo. Her nervousness over the past couple of weeks had keyed me up, and this setback slashed through the relief that came with her improvement like a switchblade. I knew from experience that she couldn't hear anything through the blood rushing, but I kept talking anyway as I slid her gently backwards. She grunted with each pant - it was like sobbing - and spread her claws out on the tiles. When her head came out, I saw her eyes pressed shut. It was worse when she opened her eyes. Though her neck was stiff with fear, her eyes darted around, showing the whites. The muscles around the rims involuntarily widened as she tried to focus on things that must have been for her like the ground coming up when you fall in a nightmare. I remembered a little kid years before in a lousy log bunker in the jungle, a little boy who had the same look Roo had now. The boy's eyes were bleeding from the concussions of artillery explosions, darting around in lantern light to see where the next thud was going to hit. Roo was in a nightmare, seeing things in the corners or on the walls or on the ceiling. Seeing things too powerful and malevolent for some little puppy to stand up to.

Down on the floor beside her I kept trying to sound upbeat about the walk. I clipped the collar on her - the same collar all the recent fosters had worn. Not so much as a collar to her name. I gave her a chance to respond to a little tug on the leash. I knew she wouldn't. As soon as I started to get up, she scrambled back under the toilet. There was no sound but her panting.

I got an arm under her and started to pick her up. She rolled onto her side and went limp, as she must have when her mother picked her up by her scruff. She folded in half sideways when I hefted her off the floor. It was the first time I picked her up since her days of not getting in the car by herself. She wasn't the same spindly dog. She wriggled a little, but when the fact that we were moving was established, she stopped. I carried her outside into the dark and put her down on the sidewalk. She went into a crouch with her head flattened out. Her neck was hard, and her eyes were wide open and glinting black in the street lights. I was on my knees on the concrete beside her, holding her, not sure what to do next. I had hoped that finding herself out for a walk would be enough of a distraction to help her walk it off. I wondered if she felt me breathing hard from carrying her. God knows I could feel her.

Suddenly, Roo's ears snapped to attention and her head came up. A backlit black cat was standing in the middle of the street. His long shadow crept across the pavement and stopped right at Roo's forepaws. She tilted her head as the impression of possibly the first cat she had ever seen queried the database passed down to her in her genes from wolves on the tundra through retrievers in Pasadena. The cat obliged Roo with more processing time by arching his back and standing his ground before he let out a big hiss. That hiss was delightful to Roo. She did a little play hop on her front paws. She forgot who she was a minute before and became the dog this puppy will grow into, up on her feet and dancing. The cat trotted away, and Roo was ready to see what other surprises were out there in the dark. About fifty feet down the sidewalk, Roo turned to look back in the direction of the cat. She looked at me and let out one big bark, the first I had ever heard from her.

It was a beautiful, deep-throated bark. It filled the night, and sounded exactly like, "ROO!"

❀   ❀   ❀

The next morning, I found out what had scared Roo. There was a window filled with green bottle glass that looked out onto the walkway beneath the air conditioner. When the handyman walked past that window, Roo ducked and scrambled. What frightened her the night before was me - my distorted shadow on that glass when I went out to check the unit.

Something was different this time. Roo didn't hide. She came to me and sat down with her flank pressed against my leg.

That was the exact moment when there was no more denying anything. I got down beside her and said, "You're the bravest puppy I ever knew, Roo. My brave, brave little girl."

Photo by Melody Platt

                              ❀   ❀   ❀

Roo had been wearing the hand-me-down
rainbow collar that came with my first Indi Lab foster
dog. Every one of them was the dog equivalent of
penniless - unnamed and out in the world without so
much as a collar. We'll be keeping that collar. The foster
dogs to come will need it. All I had on hand was an old
collar that was Orville's when he was a puppy that I have
kept with me since he died. I put it on Roo. She made a
big game of putting a collar on, which I didn't put an end
to because it was a joy to see how happy going for a walk
made her. Every time she squirmed and wrestled on the
floor when I put her collar on, it reminded me of how
close she came to dying with an IV in the arm she had
chewed through on a steel table in a shelter.

I led her out for a walk. As soon as we got on the
street, Roo gave me a tug that tore the D-ring right out of
the leather. Orville's old collar became useable as nothing
more than a remembrance of my dog in the clouds. That
was as it should have been. We went to the pet store - it
was the first time that Roo strode right through the
electric doors that had scared her so much before. Inside,
she wasn't jumpy at all. She sat patiently as I tried
different collars on her. I chose a fine red leather one that
looks pretty nestled in her golden fur. She wore it out of

the store, and if it's just a figment of my imagination that Roo wore it proudly, so be it.

I hope that when dogs die, they go someplace where they don't have to worry about us any more. Orville had to do enough of that while he was alive. A place where if they do happen to glance back once in a while, it would be to see things like the joining of a new dog to the old pack. Orville would be glad. He would not want me to be without a dog. I hope he would feel that for Roo, it was a good day, too.

✿　　✿　　✿

Roo is not healed. Roo has not been unfrightened. She is mending fast, but some of the scars from her hard puppyhood run deep. I have scars that have never smoothed out. I know how that goes.

Roo's fears now seem centered on the most fundamental thing in life: light. What she sees in the light and in the shadows, only Roo knows, but she is always seeing things that worry her. It's only bad at night, when any light switching on or off signals danger to her. Had her leash broken when a streetlight flickering in an alley made her bolt the other night, there's no knowing how far

Roo would have run. Reflections, changes in the light of any kind, frighten Roo. Curtains fluttering the light in a breeze or sunlight glimmering on leaves make Roo look for cover. It could be an effect of deprivation. It could be that lights coming on presaged something bad about to happen where she was imprisoned in the dark. We'll never know the ghosts still haunting Roo. I am trying hard to understand what is scaring my little girl so much, but it's more important to teach her that she will never be hurt again. It will take some time. Roo is not healed - she is healing. She will keep getting better

※　　　※　　　※

It is years past the time for me to go home, or at least close to home, somewhere in the Northeast where I am from. Roo won't know when she wags at me to be praised for how well she hops in the car now that we will be setting off on a 3000-mile drive. I hope that strange places won't frighten her too much. I think she will be all right.

There is no place in particular for us to go at the other end. I don't know within two hundred miles where we will live. I am inclined much more to starlight now than streetlight, and I think that's going to be fine with Roo. She will have snow in her life and rivers and ponds to swim in. This Los Angeles puppy will grow into a New England country dog. And inevitably, she will be part of the choosing.

There is only one stop I want to make along the way, a thousand miles east of here, at a small mound of rocks - or what will be left of it nine years after I built it. It sits beside a quiet trail on top of a low mesa north of Boulder, Colorado. There is a clear view of Orville's home sky all around it. It has a view of the front range of the Rocky Mountains, a few miles to the west, and, to the east, a muddy swimming hole favored by local dogs. If it is clear up at Orville's grave, you can see a hundred miles of the East Colorado prairie where Orville was born stretching to the horizon beyond that pond. You can see the first hundred miles of the prairie Roo and I will drive through after I visit Orville's grave for the last time, when we leave, with no more than a vague direction, to seek our new home.

In those hot days after Orville died, there weren't many suitable rocks to be found in that hard dirt up there. It took five days of gathering and carrying them in a canvas firewood holder to mount that humble commemoration. It marks the place loved most by a dog who appeared first in the clouds and then traveled the world. When I finished it and knelt there, the smallest bird I ever saw, like some kind of bird new to the world that very day, landed on my shoulder and sang in my ear, and that was enough to make me think it was time to die.

My dog and I will get in our little car and set off down the dirt road leading away from there and drive. I know these two things about Roo. She will lie in the passenger seat with her head on my thigh, and like me, she will be in some degree of trouble, and on her way to getting better every day.

About the Author

Brian Beker is a writer, pilot and documentary filmmaker. He is working on *The Dog in the Clouds,* a memoir about his white Labrador Orville, who appeared in the midnight storm clouds over Kathmandu two years before he was born on the Colorado prairie.

CPSIA information can be obtained at www.ICGtesting.com
Printed in the USA
LVOW01s1915231214

420153LV00030B/1321/P

9 780615 782508